UMBILICUS

Poetry and Visuals
of the Sensuous

T0163908

UMBILICUS

Poetry and Visuals
of the Sensuous

Poetry by Carrie Schiffler
Visuals by Johanna Stickland

An Imprint of
Durvile Publications

UpRoute Books

UPROUTE IMPRINT OF DURVILE PUBLICATIONS LTD.

Calgary, Alberta, Canada
www.durvile.com

Copyright © 2019 Carrie Schiffler & Johanna Stickland

LIBRARY AND ARCHIVES CATALOGUING IN PUBLICATIONS DATA

Umbilicus: Poetry & Visuals of the Sensuous
Schiffler, Carrie, author
Stickland, Johanna, artist

1. Love Poetry | 2. Erotic Poetry
3. Canadian Poetry | 4. Canadian Art

Book Four in the Every River Poems Series

ISBN: 978-1-988824-41-3 (print pbk) | ISBN: 978-1-988824-45-1 (e-book)
ISBN: 978-1-988824-46-8 (audiobook)

Cover and book design, Lorene Shyba

We would like to acknowledge the support of
the Alberta Government
through the Alberta Book Fund.

Durvile is a member of the Book Publishers Association of Alberta (BPAA)
and Association of Canadian Publishers (ACP).

Printed in Canada

First edition, first printing. 2019

Umbilicus is dedicated to the
#metoo community.
May we never cease to pursue
our brilliant body's right
to shame-free pleasure.

CONTENTS

PREFACE

I WRITE to capture that which gives me goose-bumps. I write to free my pillow from having to absorb the sobs of heartache. I write to self soothe. I write to verbally masturbate. I write to power-wash my dirty mind. I write to prove a point. I write to figure out what is said-point.

In the fall of 2018 I attempted to self publish a collection of poetry. This chapbook consisted of a dozen poems and a few poorly printed photo-graphs. It set me back thirty bucks for a single copy. Making multiples with the hope of selling them and turning a profit would have been a fools game. It was only fourteen pages! About a month later, Lorene Shyba, the dynamo of Durvile & UpRoute appeared with an offer. I was thrilled but doubted whether or not I had enough ma-terial for an actual book. She suggested I partner up with an exceptional artist. Good idea. I knew just the gal for the job. I have been a huge fan of Johanna Stickland ever since hanging some of her earliest pieces on the fridge. Now that she is all grown up, her artwork has not only matured, but it is so exquisite that it allows her to make a living doing what she loves with no need for a side hustle. I am humbled to have her images snuggled up alongside my words. It should work. We are not only connected via DNA but by lived experience as well. Both no stranger to the objectification of the male gaze, it's here we collaborate to expose, reclaim and indulge the body's need for connection. I can only hope that you, the reader, will also feel some kind of connection here within the pages of *Umbilicus* and better yet, may it bring you pleasure.

— *Carrie Schiffler 2019*

NO LONGER

I no longer awake in a stranger's bed
Thick of tongue and labial ache
No flat amber hair of the dog
Waiting beside the futon on the floor
I no longer tiptoe across a battlefield
of dead soldiers

In the morning
I was always the first one awake
Sniffing around for a way to make coffee
Or change for the bus

I no longer awake in a stranger's bed
Staring at a sleeping face and wondering
if it's love
Does he have a job
a secret
a disease
I no longer awake
With a list of apologies and
items to buy at the drug store

I no longer awake in a stranger's bed
In search of myself
Me, the meat of me
Under the covers
Between the sheets
In the embrace
Of the unknown I would be defined
Or so I thought

I no longer awake questioning
where or who I am

I no longer awake in a stranger's bed
I awake alone
Comfortable with the company I keep.

THE RECKONING

My thong is all wrong
It lost its snap fourteen washes ago
An attempt to slingshot it across the room
Lands it at my feet
Next to the cat food
The still life of spent underwear and tender vittles
Title: Feed the pussy
Always feed her first.
Back in the day when I was up for play
I couldn't go commando
My youth juice gave me away
Every time
The tell-tale snail trail
Leading Hansel to Gretel
clear, odourless
yet
Wet
rivulet
obvious
And blush-worthy
Like this poem.
And my sex life almost done
It's been a good run
With heart lifted skywards
Chest flesh draws downwards
Grateful the babies are grown
And my honey is an ass man
These once perky puppies
Are dog tired
Rest well tired tits
Your work here is done.

WORDS

He wrote poetry by candlelight
drawn to the flame
She followed him
the spark of his pen
ignited a fire down below
His word-wrangling ways were cool fingers on her spine
His poems a probe between the folds of her awakening
She let him in
opened the flood gates of her
fountain of youth
oh how he loved to frolic there
while she edited him
constantly
searching for her own voice muffled in the sheets
of paper
She lost her self
Somewhere in his eternal monologue
there was no room for her
On his one-man stage
They drifted apart to other bar rooms and bedrooms
Both of them left
but neither said goodbye.

ANCIENT WHISKEY PROPHETS

Ancient Whiskey Prophets
Can read a man by the dregs in his glass
And how the smoke lifts off a cigarette

Ancient Whiskey Prophets
Listen to the gathering clouds
And warn of bad weather

Ancient Whiskey Prophets
Feel a fight before the dogs do
And always throw the last punch

Ancient Whiskey Prophets
Sit on the shoulders of country singers
And whisper their next big hit

Ancient Whiskey Prophets
Can love a man different each night
Make him break him take him
Closer to God and the stove where he'll beg
to cook her perfect eggs.

LUNACY ON A THURSDAY NIGHT

They think I'm crazy
On the dance floor
Tearing it up
Whirling dervish style
wild
My night out
With my closest friend
The full moon
Laughing all the way
to tequila town
Ignites my fire
Lights my smoke
This round-faced accomplice
Helps me pretend
I am Canada's next top dancer
The Super Moon declares me a Super Star
I sparkle twirl shine
Light on the upturned faces
my audience of six
All of whom wish
to tango
With my madness
Good thing
This bar star only emerges once a month.

I'M IN

all in
Inwards motion and devotion to surf it like the ocean
Be flowing and towing the line to the shore
Leave it all on the floor
I'm in all in
introspective reflective a truth-seeking detective
Dig it up rig it up
Sign me up I'm down
Like an insane posse clown
I come around with crazy phrases
From old school days yes
When we be talking face to face yes
Writing with our pens not our thumbs
blood letting ink linking
brain body soul
Fill the hole in your heart
With your own self-made art
Live your masterpiece
On the daily
Sing fuck cook read
Paint dance play bleed
Are you in
In like sin?
If you're not *in* you're *out*
Out of your mind
Out of your body
Shit out of luck
I'm in all in
Come on in
Wipe your feet have a seat
Design the sacred space
between your ears
And keep the welcome mat dirty.

BRING ME YOUR ANIMALS

I want to know you better than you know you
you know
paint me a slideshow
a memory montage
of firsts
first tooth
first day at school
first wet dream
first love
first car
first grey hair
let me be the first to make you laugh so hard
you fart and cough and come a little
closer
Bring me your animals
let me wallow in your dirty laundry
while you read your journal out loud
in your best worst Eastern European accent
sing me that song that makes you cry
every time
whisper fears beneath the sheets
as I trace your scars with my tongue
I want to know you better than you know you
you know.

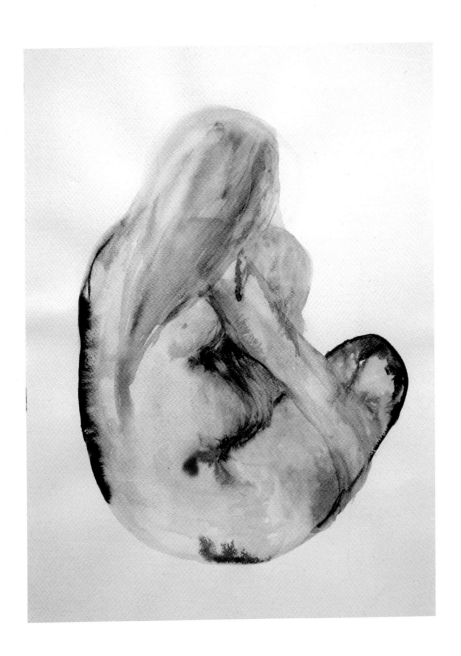

BUILT FOR THE ROAD AHEAD

Tangle dancing in a motel on wheels
Left them stiff
Head and hearts pounding
Each vying to be the first to break the sound barrier
and her spirit
Like footprints on windows
Smudging the shatterproof membrane
Of their four-door sleepless womb
Vinyl tracks on backs
Hair matted with the reek of car freshener
Pants puddled around ankles
Black bra draped across his stick
Shift
They search for clothes and words
Button mouths and shirts snapped shut
Eyes avoid mirrors and each other's thoughts
a silent blanket of to-do lists
Buy cat litter, erase browser history, drop off shame
At the bottle return
None of which they share
While outside foggy glass
The sun rises over dumpsters.

MY TRIBE

A niggling nagging gnawing
at the back door of my memory bank
I withdraw currency of stones
And blood
All red we bleed
On sheets and streets
Our meat-suits freshly pressed prints
Across a frozen lake
We hunt travel feast and frolic
On the highways airwaves forest path
mountain face sand bar and bar stools
leathered weathered warriors seekers survivors thrivers
driven by instinct and loins
to lead and follow
teachers students watchers keepers of the map
back
where the heartbeat lulls
you to cocoon in a room cushioned with the
hug of
shared stories
And past glories
scratch mark claim
stick a flag in my heart
and call me home.

THAT'S A RAP

Grrrrrl bling rapped bitch slapped job trapped
Leather biting ass kicking black cherry tart
Sugar pie puddle panty pate licker
Cum sucking hump bustin' nipple twist
Orgy gryst seeker thrill tweeker
Bubble lipped hip gripper
Give me a look a hook to pierce my skin
Draw me in
Hike your skirt lift your shirt
Rub your thighs with restless sighs
I size you up and down and round and round
The room spins when you get up to
Play the jukebox
Some junior high humpin' tune like
Bark at the Moon
And now we know your type be some
Hair flippin' air guitar wanna be rock star guy
Seizes your dreams squeezes the seams of your wallet dry
Makin' you cry for more as he slips out the door
Ozzy still sings still rings your bell
Hold tight those rebel days lest they slip away
Leaving you with a bedroom full of compromise
Lock your doubt in a cage
Engage *mula bondha* the money lock
Stock and barrel between your legs
Fire the town crier for making noise
with the boys in a no-traffic cul-de-sac kill the talk back
Hacky sac piggy back railroad track clickety clack
And sshhh little mouse clean the house

Dust-free dirt-free spit-shine empty
Bye bye gotta fly and buy me a new second-hand dress
Maybe a rubber number for my superhero psyche
To bounce from bar to bedroom and back again
to my youth
No misspending that now
This second chance dance on the lap of luxury
licking it up for free rent
And slow-cooked meals appeals to me and you
No frew frew *hausfrau* now
Bow down to the sacred cow that knows there is
no such thing
As everything is sacred therefore nothing truly is
All equal bleeding hurtling hurting beings in
sacs of skin wrapped in pretty paper
Some more in shaper than the others brothers sisters
ladies misters friends and ministers keep 'em close
Save on postage play hostess
To the biggest party of all time in your mind is a
potluck buffet
Of international delights and nights well-spent
well-meant fulfillment
If only for a twenty-second groan into a brick wall or
bathroom stall
No regrets not for rent or lease if you please
Squeeze me tease me you're the bees knees
This rap is cheese
Pass the cracker please.

FLIGHT

Sarah saw shorebirds at the seashore
and she cried
For the wings she wished she had
They skidded in to the bay
full of purpose
Tiny faces intent
On guard
Bodies strutting like teenagers on the
first day back to school
Awkward on the shifting sand
Graceful only when high
How she longed to soar with her feathered family
trusting the wind to carry her weightless
She knew how it felt
to fly.
She flew in her dreams nightly
orbiting vistas
The patchwork quilt of countrysides
the heavy metal machinations of cities
And the suburbs boring boxes

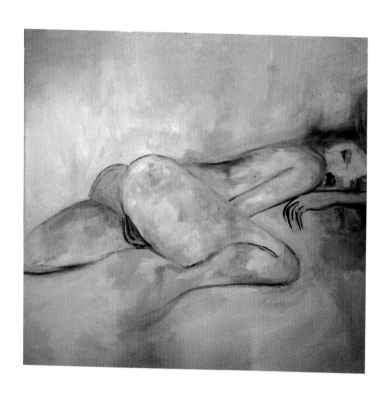

She was above it all
Untouchable
She knew how it felt
to fly.
Fearless
Unlike a child who doesn't want to sleep,
Sarah wished to never wake up.

24

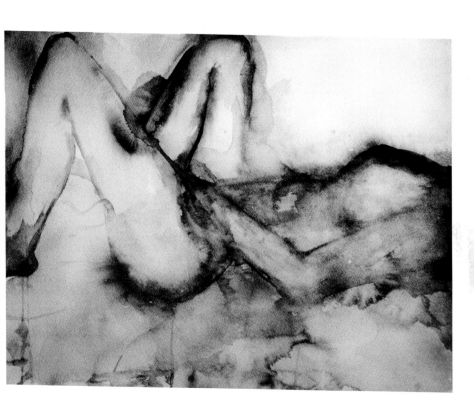

NEVER?

Never say never
say yes
like a child with an unlimited allowance
the world is your candy store
no self limitation or cheap imitation
be big or be gone
leave a mark live your song
Choose love that's the only option
put your fear up for adoption
open your eyes your mind your heart
first breath
inspiration
rise out of hibernation
no hesitation
when that warrior wants to play
let 'em see the light of day
shake hands with yourself and let the dance begin
feel the romance settle in
lock eyes with the reflection
commit to a new direction
peace waits for you there
at the corner of *trust* and *share*
Wake it up shake it up lose control
you're not going *any* where but *every* where
To be fair, you're already *there*!
I can feel it coming in the air tonight, oh Lord.
Oh God, don't bring Him into it

refund the ticket to that one-way guilt trip
stay hep, call yourself spiritual
get in touch with the ethereal
converse with spirits immaterial
hold the feather hold the rock
and roll with the punches
listen to your hunches
all the answers reside
inside let the landslide of all you can't control give way
to a new day
a new way to say
I never thought I'd…

ROCKSTAR

The moment before the big moment
Is the best moment
Guts churn a chemical stew
Of hormones and sticky liquor
Prickles skin ecstatic
Heart bangs on fear's door
with hinges rusty from
Tears
And years wasted
Watching not taking
Waiting not waking
To the gift
Splayed open
Like a playmate plump and ready
For the heady dream
To play out play in play on
The stage of my imagination
I am the star
The frontman
The lead
In this music video we call the weekend.

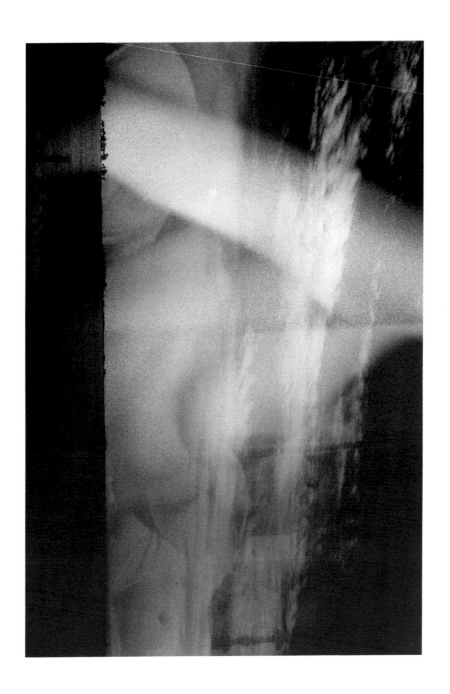

TATTOO

Blue black flesh etching needle carving
Can you feel me
My name scratched in prison ink
above your nipple
Did it hurt?

How often do you place your hand over your heart
and
remember
the beat of mine
From long ago days when we thumb wrestled
on the bus.
or
Is C-A-R-R-I-E
A mistake of bloody letters
weighing you down
the aging dregs of memory
you ignore and hide beneath the sheets and shirts
or
Have you ever stood naked in front of a mirror
And laughed at me
Backwards... E-I-R-R-A-C
Did it hurt?

69 TRIUMPH

You left nothing
but subtext and your leather jacket
Sullen and sloppily
Tossed on the bed
Speaking volumes
Of my weakness
Weak kneed
Week end needs
Has me running around
to return your hide for one last ride
Hunting you down
In all the obvious places
But you chose the road less travelled
Revving it up
In the dark alley
Of my sanity
Idling in my vanity
Motor oil slick you
Wordlessly talk me into
Giving up my underground parking.

MORNING RITUAL

Wake up lazy muse!
And amuse me, infuse me
With wit and wonder and the
horny liquor of original thought
Emerge from your sloth cocoon
Toss aside that Germanic duvet
Of efficiency
And drag those ancient bones to the alter
And the urn of black-roast battery boost
Supercharge synapses
Reverse tired to wired
Clear cut the deadwood forest of dreamland
And snap open the shades
Now, "darken the page,"
As Sir Cohen would say
Scratch bleed repeat
Scratch bleed repeat
Scratch bleed repeat
And don't look back
Until the last drop of bitter love
Is drunk
And you are spent
like a winning lottery ticket.

LIGHT

Shadow puppets on her bedroom walls
The bunny befriends the bird
a naked branch scratches the window
like the cackle of a meatless witch
The sliver of light beneath the door
She prays stays bright
tonight
no silhouette will fill the frame
she's been a good girl all day
dreaming with eyes open
a semi drives by and floods her room
with hope
Of faraway places where she's leading a parade
Of animals to freedom
just outside and down the highway
she sees her future
self
safe warm and radiant.

OPEN CALL

Their knees knocked under the gum
of their table for two
He looked at her with hang dog mouth
Flapping jokes like hot cakes
Rubbing the beat of the jukebox back and forth
forth and back on her peanut butter thigh
she spreads open to tap her flip flop
to the music in his hand
phut phut split splat
juicy feet swimming in sweat
Love liquid trickles from lips
hidden until last call
They shared sad stories of past glories
Auditioned for each other beneath the disco ball
Refracted fractured hearts on display
The show must go on
The play's the thing
They both got the part and the script of anxious
clothes
Torn and tossed to the floor
Improvising their way to the bed they create
A headboard musical
and sleep through the morning applause
of the magpie.

WHEN

All packed up before bed
With a ride scheduled to take her away
So efficiently organized
Where did that come from?
She awoke at five
No need for alarm
Scrubbed and caffeinated
She puts her empty mug in the sink before
I have a chance to tell her to do so
Remember when we found an entire set of
dishes under your bed?
I tried to hold her captive
With long-winded winding stories
I stare at the plains of her face similar to mine
Yet uniquely her own
I can't look away

I'm not ready

We hug like it's the last time

Dragging a suitcase half her size

Down the narrow stairs

I offer to help

She's got this

I crack a joke

I don't want to...

The door closes.

I check each room for forgotten things

Nothing is left behind

Just me.

No trace of Johanna

Except in the mirror

I can sometimes catch a brief glimpse

If I squint through tears.

POST COITAL MONOLOGUE

Oh my God. Oh my God that was so so…
oh my God. Sorry. Sorry for crying. I'm just.
It was just so… Yeah. You know! It's been a
long time since I've like… done it. Like with
someone. It's good to know everything still
works. Oh boy does it work.

No! No. A vow of celibacy? NO! Nothing
that extreme. I quit smoking which meant
I had to quit drinking. Cuz I can't do one
without the other. Too hard. Can't go to a
movie theatre and not have popcorn. I can't
go to a bar and not have a drink. So much for
picking up guys in bars. Just as well. Mom
always said relationships that start in the
bar end in the bar. And then I had to quit
coffee. My favourite smoke was the first one
of the day with a cup of jo, 'Whore's Break-
fast'. No more coffees for me. And next to
bars, coffee shops are the best place to pick
up. Oh, yeah, you got the artists, the musi-
cians, stay at home dads, smart guys, guys
who know how to fill out a grant applica-

tion. That's who hangs out in coffee shops. Not me. Nope. Not anymore. I don't smoke, drink, do caffeine. Once I gave up all of that, I was hooked. I was hooked on kicking things I was hooked on. It's an incredible high—conquering your addictions. I systematically kicked everything I was dependent on—sugar, red meat, swearing, step aerobics, *Coronation Street*, hair products, junk mail, junk food, junk jewellery, and finally clothes, bathing and talking. It got to the point where I was barely existing. I was simply being a simple being not wanting for anything except the wanting for not wanting anything. Very Zen. Sadly it's almost impossible to live like a monk in the city. The cops eventually picked me up. They found me up on 8th Avenue, naked and doing yoga. I was charged with busking without a license. Talk about a much-needed wake-up call. I was sent to a shrink as part of my probation. We're working on slowly re-introducing my addictions.

TABITHA, A GIRL AND HER BOX

Carrie alternates between singing and speaking while
robotically going through the motions of a table dance.
Sing

Keep your distance stay away
Don't want to hear a word you say
I've heard it all before
There's no way you can impress.
There's nothing left here to address
I'm frozen to the core.
Can't you see that what you see is what you don't get
There's a vacancy but I am not for sale or rent
I'm just another fantasy in front of you and on my knees
A blow up doll would feel more than me.

Speak

Try doing this forty times a night, six nights a week for
three years. Give or take holidays and shifts missed due
to hangovers, that's approximately 37,400 table dances.

Sing

You don't care who I am
You're just a wham bam thank you ma'am
That's all I know
You only want a part of me
The place I shave for all to see
Sit back and enjoy the show.
Can't you see that what you see is what you don't get
There's a vacancy but I am not for sale or rent
A deaf and numb fantasy trained to flirt

and born to tease

A blow up doll would feel more than me.

Speak

That's 37,400 guys who have paid to be inches away
from my... gyrations.

During those three years I was sent death threats,

I was stalked and I was raped.

Once when a bar brawl broke out, guns were drawn.

The bouncer ordered me to keep dancing. I did.

I would have peed my pants had I been wearing any.

Sing

Wipe the drool from your chin

Take your hands off of your sin

Erase the gleam in your eye

Do you think you stand a chance of playing out

this sexy dance

All I'm gonna suck is your wallet dry.

Can't you see that what you see is what you don't get

There's a vacancy but I am not for sale or rent

Go home to your wife she loves you with her life

And I betcha she feels more than me

The dance ends.

Carrie resumes talking.

I was destined to be a hardened old woman at nineteen.

Until *he* walked in.

Our eyes meet. A skittish electric blue lightening strike.

Was that a smile? Did he blush? He blushed!

Who the hell is that?! He isn't married.

He's not a pervert, a redneck, a fat cat, a tourist?

What the hell is *he*? What the hell is *he* doing here?

He doesn't fit. He's like a, a, a, what? A freak?!

Carrie approaches him.

Carrie: Can I have a french fry?

He: Ahhh, have a chicken finger.

Carrie: My name's Tabitha.

He: Really?

Carrie: No. It's Carrie.

He: I'm Eugene.

Carrie: Really?

Eugene: Unfortunately.

He's not a freak. He's a nice guy. He feeds squirrels
from his bedroom window and gives me his coat in the
rain. He once dreamed of being a concert pianist. Now
those hands play on me in me opening in me a softness
a letting go. I surrender to the fall of falling in love.

I'll give you my history.

It's the only present I have to offer.

And these rough bones you pick up and polish

and place in tiny coffins.

We bury the past alive

Beside the open grave

I feel a foot slip

I grip your hand

You vow to never let go

As we wave goodbye to Tabitha.

I quit stripping. He threw me a retirement party and gave me a Mickey Mouse watch. He was older than me, which didn't matter until we socialized with his friends.

Friends: Blah, blah, blah second mortgage, blah, blah, blah more to the gallon, blah, blah, blah so tell me Carrie. What is it you do for a living?

Carrie: I, I, I'm studying actually. Yeah. I'm studying genetic engineering. I'm currently rerouting my gene pool to erase all effects of post-traumatic white-trash disorder.

Usually he forewarned his peers to avoid the whole job topic thing. I stayed quiet, except for when we were alone. He swept me off my feet, shook me upside down until all of the shit, fear and rage came spilling out. He cleaned up after me so well that when I turned to look inside, I was a brand new show home. Shiny and empty.

I wish I could burn the past

Pack it up in cardboard boxes

Ship it to outer space

I wish I could bury the past

My tears and sweat fertilizer for new growth

I wish I could use the past as target practice

Shooting each misgiving misfortune mistake

In the heart | And revel in the release of blood

No longer mine | I cannot forget

I cannot let go | Yet I can try

To forgive | One single memory at a time

Like a miser on his death bed

Handing over a penny for every last breath granted.

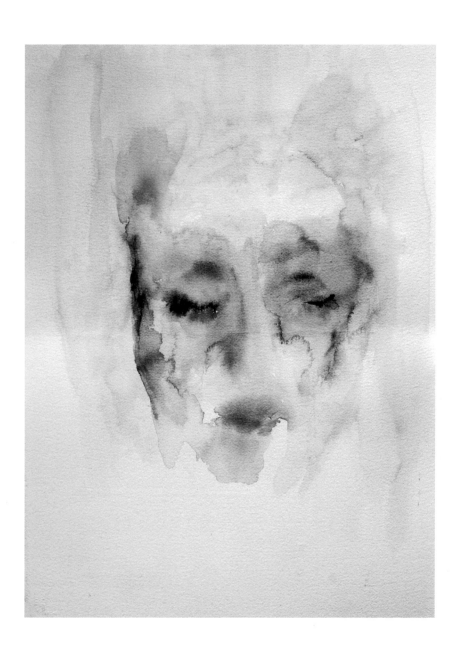

ANOTHER EXCERPT
from *Tabitha a Girl and Her Box*

I never get turned on.
No one in the audience turns me on.
Sometimes I look for that look.
That look that says, you don't belong here.
That would turn me on.
I like meeting men in pubs.
Fully clothed.
I write in my notebook pretending to be a novelist,
while jotting down a grocery list.
Anonymity excites me.
Maybe because I grew up under the
weight of strangers.
Regardless
The first taste of unexplored skin is the
most alive moment.
A lick of someone new.
Salty, sweet, sour, bitter each flavour
Targets a different part of the mouth they say.
Feeling their essence with my tongue
Their genetic history absorbed on a non-verbal voyage
straight to my primordial stew.
Never underestimate the power of a kiss.

EAT

I like to watch his index finger
on the back of a fork
firmly pressing
into flesh
raising a dripping morsel.
I envy that rare flesh
as it plays inside the rumpus room of
his perfect mouth.
His head bobs in rhythm with his chewing
His eyes a Mediterranean twinkle that flash
brief stay on remote island
I can't afford to go there
my passport has expired.
But I can look and long and pretend to
be the fork in his hand in his mouth
resting by his elbow.
Looking up expectantly
waiting to be picked up and used again.
mmmm mmmm
how he masticates.

FOUNDATION

She couldn't leave the house
without her foundation
a liquid mask
a buffer
a bumper
a shield
a disguise
"beige sunset"
was her cover up for over twenty years now
she bought her face by the case
applied it with loving artistry
with her right hand
while the other held a smoke
morning ritual
war paint
ready to battle another round
of office politics
never giving up hope
that this could be the day
someone would say
I see *you*.

ODE - NOT! - to WHY.

Stupid word, why.
One syllable
A challenge
Why.
Annoying
Why do you ask, why?
Why
loaded question
Why
Offensive
Why
Exhausting
Three little lettered W-H-Y
Claws at my locker of knowledge
I lost the key years ago
shut out
Why?
No deep thinking here
I got nothing
But puns and nonsense
WHY?
Facebook
Feeding my addiction for instant gratification
And goat videos
Why?
Prying leads to lying

Why
makes me feel like a cat petted backwards
Why?
Agitation
Regurgitation of what you want to hear
Why
Why bother
Ask me why
And you'd better be honky fucking dorey with
Why not.

HOME FOR DINNER

Ooohh
Adoration admiration infatuation fascination
Glitter tickles eyes alive
Sequined sinew sways plays sashays
amaze-*zing*
Trance Sequence
Vibrations thrummin' hummin' strummin'
Enraptured captured pulse
Captured pulse
In the man vein
Of your candy cane

Spittle leaks from the cracks
As she snaps her back
Poised and coiling
Blood now boiling
Limbs stretched beyond imagination
No time for contemplation
It's just a feeling that keeps you reeling
and silently squealing
Tongue swells to meet the treat
Of her sugar meat
You feel the heat
But maintain refinement contain confinement
Detain excitement
Recline decline
Define what your vows meant

What the wife said
Get yourself together
Ignore the lace and leather
Stuff your hands in your pocket
Tame the love rocket
Bring it on home boy
Bring it on home
Bring it on
Bring it
Bring it on back to me
Baby.

PSY*CAT*DELIC

Communication with Cooper comes at night
After an incredible edible
Opens heart chakra
I lie down
Cat climbs up to knead my belly
Massaging tummy chakra of emotions
Finally settling heavy .
Heart to heart belly to belly fur to flannel
and we talk
Wordless
Gently he instructs me
To see what I want in all its technicolour detail
Smell it feel it hear it
Manifest the life I want be the being I want to be
When doubt disturbs the daydream he tells me
I am my thoughts
The writer of the code that controls this meat suit
Switch confusion to clarity
Self loathing to loving
Fear to strength
Judgment to observation

Worry to wisdom
He convinces me I have all the answers
Inside
Excavate meditate initiate
The change I wish to be
Cooper is a healer
And I listen to the message within
his psy*cat*delic purr.

PROTECTION

They made a mess of his new deck
Partying it up out there
Squawking loud all hours of the morning
Up before his cock even

It was time to scare 'em off
A gunshot blast oughta do 'er

He rose with the crows when the inky night sky
began its bleed from black to blue
Padded out back in his house slippers
rifle ready loaded
on caffeine thud thud
heart pounding
a stirring down below
reminding him who wears the pants 'round here
He's the man
A man in control
A man protecting the all-weather stain from the
ravages of
guano

Aiming high
His thick finger squeezes the trigger
Ka-Booooooooooom
The echo of the blast continues beneath
the fluster of flapping wings
like a million bedsheets snapped overhead

He sits and waits for silence
the sign of a job well done
Eyes closed, leaning back
the hum of powerlines and important trucks
a reassuring lullabye

Cockadoodle Doooooooooo!!!!
so startled was he that he almost shot
his foot clean off
swearing, he makes his way back inside
the missus hands him toast.
Says the crows don't bother her.
"I always rise with your cock.
You know me."
Now go lock up that silly gun and sit with me awhile.
Pulling up his pants he does as he's told.
Happily ever after.

POOL BOY

When I'm rich and famous will you
be my pool boy?
You don't have to clean it.
Just stay wet.
Drip your way across the marble
Leave your flip flops outside
My door-less bedroom
Swing me gently in cocoa butter
Make my hammock rock
And roll me over till I'm golden
Even
Eat fruit off the small of my back
And I'll lap up the puddles from your
collarbones or
Wherever
Offering you money
You refuse to accept
The pleasure's all mine
You'll say, I must leave now
But you never do.

PHOTOGRAPHY

retracing steps
of yesterday's hike
for what was lost
blaming the other
for holes in pockets and
communication
silence hovers like a bird of prey

Each snapped twig, an accusation
they go their separate ways
a solo search for the same thing
the ring, that damned ring
was all she wanted
or so she thought
raising her camera to catch
capture something to behold
To be held
He stops
In the damp space she left behind
he fills his lungs with her
And for the first time he sees with his heart
the cedars
scarlet roadmap skin
touching hands to trunk
stroking

Ancient veins
He listens with his fingers
leans into the embrace
And hugs the fucking tree
they share a sigh
She feels through her lens
Their embrace from afar
This exchange
Up close
Close up
Zoom
Focus
Click
She fills her frame with him.
Herself with him
Forever fixed.

FRINGE

There was a party last night that lasted a week
And I wear my hangover stained and stuffed
In the front pocket of my memory
Remember the clown with purple teeth juggling
Balls, a smoke and a Big Gulp
The hippies henna, hemp and hump each other man
Teenagers peddle junk food for acne medication
Remember the too-familiar smell of the beer tent
And the lady who traded yoga for pints
Betcha she's sore today
Yup
Remember not sleeping head to foot in the flophouse
Of crazy cats
Hungry and restless scratching
For a playmate
All are fat and fed and frolicked out
The circus has left town
Only stains in the grass remain
Three a.m. sighs its toxic twitch
And the actors grope their way to rehab
Remember.

FROM SLAPPER TO CLAPPER

Deep red roads
criss cross country
legends in the palm of my hands
proud of the stories etched here
history and mystery past and future
country paths and downtown traffic
it's all there, here in flesh carved
Fingerprints
Tracing us back to crime scenes
shake my naked hand
soft elegance on the outside rough
and ready on the inside
Embrace my duality
please
Ask about the scars
it's okay
they don't hurt anymore
these silver ribbons
Connect the dots of liver spots
And memories
Of fun in the sun
Excessive applause
High fives and low lives
I've held them all in these hands of time.

REMEMBER

He drops in to claim a blanket on the floor
whenever the inner compass isn't sunk
in a booze-soaked funk
spends his days chasing bullets
down memory lane
fighting to forget
the fear on the faces at the end
of his gun
at the end of his innocence
at the end of his rope
swings a fresh red poppy
and the pendulum sways
he remains
still
Not reaching for its sad red beauty
Still
waiting
Not for a hand out
But for a way out and back inside
Still waiting
for someone
to cross the line
someone to open their arms
Open their door
and welcome him
home to peace.

74

I HATE JAZZ

A searing squawk from a saxophone
Blasts a hole through my chest
Circus of frantic horns
Death dirge of trumpet whine
Eviscerates me
Fuck me
God
How
I hate
Jazz
Knowing this is irrational I stay and
Listen
Music is in there somewhere?!
Not for me to hear
Only to feel?
Perhaps
Quiet intimate
Relief is the only rescue from this poly rhythmic hell
Slippery digits
Tap a familiar tempo
Under the table a
Very private dance in my pants
Whets my appetite and makes me an
X-rated be-bop she boppin' record scratchin'
Yes YES YESSSSSS
Zoo-diddy do wop zee diddler!

SPIRAL

Just one she tells herself
it's been a long week.
Just one she tells herself
and the bartender
familiar with her poison pours in silence
just one
It's been a long week I deserve it
this weather the traffic my boss the kids the bills
Trump
Just one
I work hard I owe it to myself
take the edge off
slake quench calm
drown
BUZZZZZZZZzzzzzzzzzzzzzzzzzzzzzzzzzzzzzzzz
two gulps in
trips the alarm inside her skull
warning
Go Home Go Home Go Home
flip the switch shut it up turn it off
stop the nuisance the nagging
the niggling naysayer
"Just one.
Just one more
I mean it this time."
and the bartender sets her up.

COWBOY

Whiskey promises
Slip sideways from leather lips

Rusty spurs on
electric razor waitress
Hot for gun

and lengthy
sky music

He gives her a buck
and the key to his horse.

DON'T FALL IN LOVE WITH A STRIPPER

The first time she stripped for him by candle light
A perfection so profound
He cried
Like one does when the eyes and
heart meet for the first time
Sweet pain of knowing
He could never hold her still
Never be enough for her travelling legs
Her skin illuminated
a movie montage of love letters, shared bubble baths,
picnics and pillow fights
Through an imagined soundtrack of headboard music
Her body in the candle light
Told epic tales
flirty and filthy
She spanned the genres from Euro porn to
Hollywood Rom-Com.
All a little much for his indie art film life
Where no one shared the popcorn
And everyone wore the low-budget badge of honour
He let her go without a fight
Wished her swashbuckling adventures and
an appreciative audience
But not before she danced one last time
To his soft applause.

IN THE WAKE

When things fall apart
Some people
Drink a ceremonious 40 of Crown Royal
And cry themselves sober
When things fall apart
Some people
Get a drastic haircut and take up a trendy
new ancient religion
When things fall apart
Some people
Hold the razor close and
Dream up eulogies
When things fall apart
Some people
Point fingers and demand a refund
When things fall apart
Some people
Wade through the debris
And write poetry.

WOOD

I once had a lover who cut lumber for a living
he smelled of honest labour
fresh cut cedar
And the promise of a country home
I wouldn't let him shower first
keep your jacket on
a deep throat demand
let me slip into your dusty rough flannel
while you work my knotty bits
start the slow seesaw
In my axe wound
I once had a lover who cut lumber for a living
He knew how to handle his wood
and so did I.

WORK

For eight hours
she mustered a muscled smile
that left her exhausted
crawling into a bath
she composed
speeches that would never be heard
won battles that would never be fought
fuelled by cold beer
and hot water
unwinding
tension spirals down the drain
yet she frets
and scrubs
the tub naked
with powder that stings her eyes
and makes her hands raw
dinner is the next task
longing for red meat she makes a righteous salad
instead
thriving on a steady diet of denial.

VLT'S VIBRATING LUCKY TONIGHT

Smooth round royal *heads*
Wildlife animal *tails*
Burning for the socket
Plunging hand in pocket
Fingering a toonie a loonie to toss at her kahooney
Not again not again
Never again you promised
On your wallet to your wife
To your shrink on your life
But *there she waits*
All shiny noise
Calling you
Singing slot
Makes you sweat and forget
The last time she took your last dime
There's no peace of mind
She's got you in a bind
What do you hope to find
Whip it out
Toss it in
It's your last chance
You have to win
Whip it out toss it in
It's not a lap dance
It's not a sin
You're a big boy
You make the pay
A hard workin' man
You've earned the right to play
This could be your lucky day
Whip it out toss it in.

PEELIN' RAP

The first chord of classic rock
Drugs my body like an aftershock
Shoot me up onto the stage
You got the key baby
Open my cage
I be your good girl, prom girl, take home to Mom girl
Like that chick in that flick by Adam Egoyan
I be so innocent you'll find me annoyin'
I be your wild girl your bad girl your nasty mad girl
I'll talk like a trucker make your toenails curl
Hold on to your seat
I gonna greet you treat you fresh meat in heat you
Rare medium well done
Anyway you like I'll come
'cuz it's ripe for the plucking and sucking
Blood pumping thighs thumping this pole
I'm humping
Look at me look at me tell me what you see
One fine lady I be da gravy
Look at *me* look at *me* tell me what you see
No touchin' now I'm just a fantasy.

HUNG

Meanwhile in a suburban bedroom
She scuttles along the slippery slope of memory bank
Scared of falling into shattered fragments
Of last night's puzzle
She picks her way
Through the morning-after muck
To piece together
Who deserves apologies
Floating briefly on the river of denial
Only to crash
Headfirst
Into a gully of guilt
Gasping and grasping
Fists of white water
To wash clean
Make new
A survivor
this time
Is the last time
She told herself
Again
Climbing up the crumbling foundation
Of yesterday's promise
She emerges
And cancels the invites to her pity party.

AGAVE

She ran away to Mexico to find herself
And she did
There she was at the bottom of a mezcal bottle
A pickled worm of a woman
Lying floating waiting
For a brave one to take her on take her in
Take a bite
Slide inside enjoy the ride
Till the morning after
Leaves you mourning after
Her
And the medicine chest beckons
"Follow the yellow sick road follow the
yellow sick road."
Follow follow follow follow
Follow the trail of clothes young Hansel
Back to your parents basement
While she continues her search
For weightless souvenirs.

SIGH and SIZZLE

The bleach blond beach babe bounces in
A one woman parade of bubbles boobs gum and giggles
What an entrance
"I'd like to enter her"
Mumbles from within
The applause of hands stuffed into front pockets
Whistles stifled by Bud Wiser's long necked hard Mouth
A moment of silence for all to savor the *crack*
Of nutshells beneath her stiletto

CrunchCrunch CrunchCrunch CrunchCrunch

Eyes find her seat before she does
Plunging the high cushion with her own
Smothered in pink Lycra
She leans forward to order the bartender around
Benson Hedges his bet he'll be taking her home tonight
"One look at her and I can see right through to her bedroom
All red sheets and them fancy vanilla candles."
Benson laughs a smoke pod beneath his
Wheat-pool cap, catching Blondie's eyes
Hoisted in a Walmart Wonderbra rip off
Cross My Darts
She can't resist anything cheap
Taking a light from Benson
A match struck
A strike made
A chorus of rounds
And round and round they'll go
Round the block they've both been
Both seen | Same red lights
Never green
They've heard and had the slamming door
And felt their face on this bar room floor.

SHE'S BAAA-AACK

It's in these rare silent moments she remembers
the hunt
the chase
the ritual
the war paint
It all comes back
while stealing stillness with a mug of tea
watching squirrels through the window
It's better this way
she tells herself
safer
no one gets hurt
doctors cured her good
retrained her brain to left hemisphere gain
she remains fixed
put in her place
no trace of the wild one
cleansed of feral funk
and introduced to junk
food for the skin
lavender lime lotion
pink potpourri potion
protect and prevent her ancient musk from rousing
the dormant decadent devouring diva
she once was she was once
a force to be reckoned with but now sleeps
with drugged eyes open
protecting
family and kin
from herself.

CARVE

Swivel grind sticky slinky
Slip of a hip touch of the lip
Dangerous curves ahead
Fender bender blender whirling dervish
Divine sublime
Dance out of your pants and into mine
Dance yourself silly
Dance yourself sane
Dance yourself back to source again
Carve shapes in the space between you and me
Two hearts a bridge and maybe a tree
For me to climb and watch from above
This mating ritual your dance of love.

MEAL TICKET

Her faulty shovel only digs up fools gold
And the white picket fence is too hard to keep clean
Till death do us part impossibly long.
Her marriage a merger
The mirage but a mirror
Reflecting tears where the stars in her eyes
use to shine
The dust of nuclear family fall out
Settles
on scrambled empty nest egg
Should she cash in her meal ticket for an
Endless lineup at the all-you-can-eat buffet?
Or pawn her ring for a flight somewhere warm,
new boots or
perhaps a Bengal cat
She can't decide.
Maybe once she's climbed Mt. Laundry
The answer will reside on the other side.

PREPARE

I'm so glad we made it this far
She sighed into his shoulder
Before they even left the ground
Weighed down with baggage
and endless lines
he scanned the gate for terminal kindness
and found her
the last to board or be bored
coaxing words from a reluctant puzzle
she looked up
caught by him
and he by her in that forever second
they held one another
securely fastened by flights of fancy
Wordlessly gliding to their seats
side by side pinkie fingers locked
all fears stowed
no two have never been more prepared for take off.

Carrie Schiffler is an actor who writes. Her one-woman show *Tabitha, A Girl and Her Box* depicted the three years she spent table dancing across Canada. When not writing or performing her own work, Carrie works in film and television on production such as *Murdoch Mysteries, Heartland, Bad Blood,* and *Northern Rescue* (Netflix). Her poetry has been published in *Instant Anthology, Spare Change, Bemused* and *Downtown L.A. Life.*

Johanna Stickland is a Canadian painter, photographer and writer based in Portugal. Johanna's painting and photographic work has been featured in numerous publications including *Girl on Girl: Art and Photography in the Age of the Female Gaze, EXIT Magazine, Vision Magazine,* and *Metal Magazine.* Her work is held in collections across the world including Australia, France, Canada, the United States and Germany.

UpRoute

Every River Poems Series

Series Editor: Lorene Shyba

A Wake in the Undertow: Rumble House Poems
Rich Theroux & Jessica Szabo

Living in the Tall Grass: Poems of Reconciliation
Chief R. Stacey Laforme

Vistas of the West: Poems and Visuals of Nature
Foreword: Doris Daley
Editors/Curators:
Lawrence Kapustka, Susan Kristoferson, Lorene Shyba

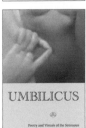

Umbilicus: Poetry and Visuals of the Sensuous
Carrie Schiffler & Johanna Stickland